Triage for the Stuck Church

Dr. Steve Smith

Triage for the Stuck Church

ISBN: 978-1-941000-14-4

For information contact; www.churchequippers.com

Contents

Introduction

*They didn't teach me anything
about that in seminary.*

Has that thought ever crossed your mind? We all started ministry somewhere. No matter where it was, we faced a learning curve.

My introduction to being a pastor was in rural Wisconsin in a town with a population of less than 2000. I was fresh out of training and had no idea what I was in for. But I got a taste of it the night my wife and I arrived in town for the formal search team interview. Not knowing where the church building was located, I stopped at the four corners gas station and asked where the Baptist church was. The attendant looked at me blankly, then called over his shoulder to others in the building. "Does anyone know where the Baptist church is?" The collective response was "No."

My wife and I wandered the streets looking for our destination—this was, after all, a very small town. The church was two blocks from the station! It sunk in right away. This congregation's local footprint answered the uncomfortable question, "If your church closed its doors, would anybody in your town miss you?" with "Not at all." I accepted the call to be their pastor anyway and spent ten years loving and leading the people of that congregation.

By the time I left 10 years later the church's impact on the town had changed. The church had grown significantly from the fifty attenders I found when I arrived. The congregation had gained a reputation of being compassionate, taking in hurting people and seeing them come alive with the gospel. We built a new building on the edge of town and helped another new congregation get established in our old building.

During the years at this church, I had many 'they didn't teach me anything about that in seminary' moments—particularly about how to build church ministry systems. More importantly, they never taught me which systems are the critical indicators of church health. I had to find that out by trial and error.

I matured though the lessons I learned while redeveloping that first congregation. I went on to plant a thriving church in Florida, then spent a decade and a half coaching church planters and established church pastors as the southeast regional leader for Converge.

I found that most pastors do not know what to address when they come to the place of asking, "Why is my congregation stuck and going nowhere?" They sense there is still life in the congregation. They notice that there are lost people all around them that need the gospel. They are not ready to throw in the towel and walk away from their church family just yet. But they are not happy that they do not know what to do.

Perhaps you are one of these pastors. You have worked at leading your congregation to new growth. You have tried a number of tactics; special meetings, new programs for children and youth, outreach events, prayer times to pray that God would spark a hunger for the lost in His people. You have worked to improve your preaching skills and chosen sermon topics that will speak to a wider audience. Perhaps you have changed the church's name, updated the worship style and adapted to the local culture. Maybe you personally have become a presence in the community, going to local Chamber of Commerce meetings, becoming a chaplain for the police or fire departments, coaching a local sports team, or lending your abilities as a counselor to help troubled people outside the church. But the church still has not grown.

To top it all off, possibly a new church has opened its doors close by. You have seen as you passed by on Sundays how people from your neighborhood are going there—people you wish would come to your church.

Or maybe you are the new pastor of a church. You have found out, like I did, that the church is friendly but unready to grow. Note that I said unready, not unwilling. They may also be unwilling, but that is because they have lost sight of who they are in Christ.

Am I hitting a nerve? You are pastoring a church that is essentially inward-focused. The attenders love being together or, at least, are stuck together by history, theology or proximity. They probably will stay together until members move away or die and the survivors have to close the doors. They may be glad you are their pastor but they're nowhere close to being ready to be a thriving church. And you may not have the foggiest idea how to change the church's direction because they didn't teach you anything about that in seminary.

The Need for Church Triage

Your ministry to them doesn't have to continue being like this. What I want to share with you in this short eBook is a triage process by which you can discover what is at the heart of what is wrong for your church. What this triage will do is help you face where you need help and direct you where to find help to redevelop your congregation into a healthy, outward-focused church.

Triage is a term created by doctors for medics on the battlefield who were the first to deal with the wounded and dying. They recognized that not all the men they were handling were going to recover. So, they invented protocols to sort the wounded into categories: those lightly wounded whose medical treatment could be delayed, those who had to have immediate help there at the medical tent in order to survive and those who needed to be made comfortable because they were not going to make it. The triage process looks at identifiable signs so that a decision of what to do with the wounded person can be made as rapidly as possible.

A church triage process involves looking at identifiable signs in certain critical systems to see what they reveal about the congregation's health. If some of these systems are broken, rebuilding them will be your first step in renewing the church. If all of these critical systems are down, the church is moving toward death.

Just by knowing this harsh reality can give you the direction, empowered by the Spirit, in which to lead the congregation. A local congregation is more resilient than a dying human body because Jesus, who reigns over his Church, is in its midst. He can breathe life back into the congregation. Jesus has the power to change their minds and hearts. And he is willing to use you as his undershepherd to bring this about. Do not forget that.

Which systems are critical for understanding the level of health in your church?

If you look closely at any church, you will discern the presence of eighteen distinct systems. They may not share the same outward features, but structurally, they function to accomplish exactly the same things. These systems can be grouped into five categories.

DNA Systems: These are the three foundational systems of any church. They define the future direction and strategies that will guide this church. Vision is the bedrock upon which all the other systems will be built. The Leadership of the church has to be in agenda harmony with this vision. Agenda harmony clears the way for collaborative Decision Making so that leaders can move forward together.

Core Systems: These five Systems—Evangelizing, Discipling, Gathering, Connections and Leadership Training—provide the lifeblood of the church. These systems are core because they define the primary work of the leaders in developing a congregation. Making disciples who pursue intimacy with God is the principal function of Christ's church. How people come to faith, grow in that faith and become part of the congregation, as well as begin participating in its mission is defined by these systems.

Stabilizing Systems: Two systems—Finances and Facilities—make it possible for a congregation to become established in a community. Every church body must have a home, even if it is using rented facilities or some public area. All churches handle money for some reason, either for its operational costs, for missions, for paying God's servants or a combination of all of these. These systems help the church stabilize its place in its community and maintain its ongoing presence.

Body Life Systems: All congregations have their own way of pursuing intimacy with God together. These five systems—Shepherding, Spiritual Life, Teaching, Communication and Community Relationship—tie the people of the congregation together with God, each other and the community in which they live and where they have been called to sow and water the gospel.

Growth Systems: If you have been around churches for any length of time, you know how people come in the front door and go out the back door of the church. It takes more than a good worship gathering to hold onto people who attend. People connect deeply to a church through its Small Groups, Ministries and Missions. These systems fuel the ongoing growth of a church body.

Now take a breath. I am not going to suggest that you need to examine all eighteen in this triage. That would be discouraging and a waste of time. In reality, triage for a stuck church involves looking at only Five Critical Systems. Other systems can be problematic as well, but they are only symptoms of being unhealthy, not the root cause of unhealth.

The Five Critical Systems

The five systems that matter for your evaluation are Spiritual Life, Vision, Evangelizing, Discipling and Leadership Training. These five are the core builders of church health. All other systems are linked to them. These are the starting point of church renewal. They empower your church to make and retain more disciples. Here is a brief summary of each.

Spiritual Life

This system should be considered the life pulse of the church, even above its Vision. It is how people come to know God and respond to His leading over the congregation. It addresses how people live in freedom and worship passionately their Abba Father. While it is included as one of the Body Life Systems, Spiritual Life is foundational for all the systems, even the church's Vision. When leaders pay tireless attention to this system, it is what makes the congregation alive. Without a healthy spiritual life system, the church will eventually crack and splinter when spiritual warfare gets hot and people's sin is exposed.

Often churches assume that spiritual life is not a system and believe that it will happen naturally. While there is truth to this belief, the function of a Spiritual Life System is to make sure the church is engaged regularly in spiritual disciplines that will encourage people to pursue deeper intimacy with God. Times of prayer, fasting and other such activities cannot be only spontaneous; they need to be planned and initiated in appropriate settings within the body life of the church. Training people in how to keep in step with the Spirit is an essential foundation of a Spiritual Life System. Also, knowing how to restore those caught in sin is a critical part of this system. Essentially, a healthy Spiritual Life System is about the intentional ways you will engage with God to enhance spiritual life in your attenders.

When the Spiritual Life System is neglected, there is an increase in: 1) Apathy towards God's reign and worship; 2) Counseling demands; 3) Prayerlessness in the congregation; and 4) Sin crisis in people, including the leaders.

Common church substitute for Spiritual Life: Excitement and Spiritual Experiences.

Vision

When I was learning how to lead a church, vision stood for what kind of church model you wanted to imitate. It represented the best ideas about how to do church effectively in one's community and came with a three-to-five year plan. For some pastors, vision is a number as in, "We are going to reach 100 new people this year." Or they talk in terms of their church's preferred future.

What vision is to Jesus is quite different. He was twisted with compassion when he saw the crowds because they were as confused and helpless as sheep without a shepherd (Matthew 9:36). Jesus' response is the essence of vision. Vision is what moves you to compassion and proclamation of the gospel as a result of seeing the great needs of the people in the community where God has sent you. It comes to a leader or a team through prayer and observations about the community, as well as the church's resources and passion.

Like Paul's dream at Troas of the Macedonian man begging for help, vision is a revelation from God and not your best ideas or your personal preferences. It tells you why God has your congregation in your community at this time; why your church exists for the sake of the Kingdom. Discovering God's vision for your local congregation will guide you and the congregation in developing a strategy to reach the people in your community.

When the Vision System is neglected, there is an increase in: 1) Aimless activities. 2) Lack of engagement by leaders in effective outreach; 3) Stagnated growth; and 4) Competition for church resources.

Common church substitute for Vision: A Personalized Theological Definition of the Church.

Evangelizing

Evangelizing is half of the Great Commission, the part that is the proclamation of the good news about Jesus. An Evangelizing System is not about whether or not you, the leader, personally are able to share the good news about Jesus, either through your preaching or witness. The function of this system is to help the church to become evangelistically effective. This means more than creating an evangelistic approach. It is creating an evangelizing culture where all the people in your congregation live to share the gospel with those around them intentionally through their lives and words, because they are full to overflowing with gratitude for what God has done for each of them though Jesus.

The primary question the Evangelizing System is asking and then answering is: "What are the faith-sharing connection points between lost people and the people who make up this congregation?" It is estimated that less than 5% of all Christians in the USA ever lead anyone to faith in Jesus. One of the contributing factors to this unhappy statistic is that most Christ-followers have few non-believers as their friends. Non-believers known by your attenders are accorded very little relational time, as most believers prefer the society of other Christians. Changing this reality is a primary part of developing a healthy Evangelizing System.

The second question this system addresses is: "How does this congregation work together to reach lost people with the gospel?" A church that does not have a game plan for evangelizing the lost together is engaging in wishful thinking, because most people need the structure of a team in order to stay engaged in evangelism. A healthy church has more than one strategy and encourages segments of the congregation to develop strategies for their workplace, neighborhood and city. Whatever strategy the church pursues, this system is clearly at the center of the congregation's fulfilling its vision. All strategies that the church develops should bear that in mind, so that the people for whom they have compassion are at the focus of these strategies.

When the Evangelizing System is neglected, there is a decrease in: 1) Baptisms; 2) Prayer for the lost; 3) People inviting people; and 4) Passion for the gospel.

Common church substitute for Evangelizing: Big Push Days.

Discipling

Discipling is the second half of the Great Commission. Clearly, merely guiding someone to believe and be baptized is not the end of the process of making disciples. Like evangelizing, your ultimate goal is to create a discipling culture, where everyone—child, teen and adult—is not only seeking to grow in their knowledge of God and His grace, but is putting it out there for all younger believers as well. Although you may develop teaching components for certain parts of your process, people learn to follow Jesus from other followers.

In truth, churches are discipling people, but not in a way that produces great results. Instead of a carefully thought through approach that recognizes what it means to teach new believers to obey everything Jesus taught us, both through the Word and through living it out before them, many churches' discipling process has a catch-as-catch-can feel to it. With no clear guidelines, each new believer has to figure out for him or herself what they need to know. For many, they just look at the lives of the other church attenders and within six months, they have learned all they think they need to know.

This is a major reason why developing your Discipling System is so critical. Many people who are currently populating your church have not been well discipled. This is not just true of young believers. People in major leadership roles often have serious deficiencies in their learning to obey everything Jesus taught. When you realize that the goal of discipling is to lead believers towards ongoing transformation into the image of Jesus, then you will begin to take the development of your discipling approach very seriously. It should never be left to chance nor should you believe that the disciple will discover what he or she needs to know without your guidance.

When the Discipling System is neglected, there is a decrease in: 1) Maturing believers; 2) Potential leaders; 3) Consistency of Christian walk; and 4) Cohesiveness of congregation.

Common church substitute for Discipling: Lectures.

Leadership Training

No church can continue to grow without more leaders, because it is first having more leaders, not more people, that fuels growth. Having people trained and willing to take charge over vital ministries is essential to healthy church growth. The central function of this system is to allow the leaders to embrace their biblical function of equipping others for the works of service so that the body of Christ might be built up (Ephesians 4:12). There is an emphasis on on-the-job training, as new leaders are not made in the classroom, but in the field. Yet classroom training is also essential, allowing each new leader to gain understanding about his or her own spiritual life, leadership skills they can use and people skills so they can handle different types of people in an appropriate manner.

This is the one system that must be led by the pastor and the top leadership of the church and not assigned to a coordinator. It is from the leaders of the church that new leaders learn how God wants them to lead. It is a task that the pastor must give at least 25% of his time.

When the Leadership Training system is neglected, there is a decrease in: 1) Church growth (because growth starts with more leaders rather than more people); 2) Functioning systems; 3) Pastor's free time; and 4) Multiplication of ministries.

Common church substitute for Leadership Training: Using Warm Bodies While Waiting for Leaders to Come through the Door.

The Triage Evaluation

To take this evaluation, you will need to check your records or quiz your congregation to answer some of the categories. Honesty is a gift to yourself, so properly count what needs to be counted. For example, when you answer the Vision evaluation section on 'Written Vision,' survey your attenders to find out exactly how many of them actually know what the vision is instead of guessing. Your best guess may be wrong. Remember, this is to help you know what needs to be addressed so that you can begin to lead your congregation toward health.

You can do this evaluation alone. But I encourage you to do it with your top leadership team to get a clearer picture of the health of each system. Invite them to meet with you, giving them each a copy of the Triage (you are allowed to make copies of the Triage Evaluation for your team). Have them each evaluate the Five Critical Systems. Then compare the results together. Average out your team's totals to determine your systems' health. This process can be completed in thirty minutes and can give your leaders a sense of urgency about addressing their church's health.

In each section, choose the statement that best describes your church. At the end of each section, add the point values of all the statements and divide the total by the number indicated to score that system. When you are finished, transfer your scores to the Final Evaluation section.

Spiritual Life System Evaluation

Healthy Outcome: Disciples demonstrate passion for God and His Kingdom.

Practiced Regularly

1 ____ The church regularly practices worship and Bible study.

3 ____ Besides worship and Bible Study, the church has a regularly scheduled prayer time together.

5 ____ Besides worship, Bible study and a regular prayer time, the church teaches intimacy with God through spiritual disciplines.

Growth of Prayer Involvement

1 _____ The church has no way of measuring how many attenders are involved in prayer for the people and ministry of the church.

2 _____ 10% of the attenders participate in some form of prayer time in the life of the church.

3 _____ 25% of the attenders participate in some form of prayer time in the life of the church.

4 _____ 50% of the attenders participate in some form of prayer time in the life of the church.

5 _____ 75% of the attenders participate in some form of prayer time in the life of the church.

Counseling Load

1 _____ The church leaders see 1 out of 4 attenders or more sometime during the year for more than one session of counseling (couples count as two).

2 _____ The church leaders see 1 out of 5 attenders sometime during the year for more than one session of counseling (couples count as two).

3 _____ The church leaders see 1 out of 8 attenders sometime during the year for more than one session of counseling (couples count as two).

4 _____ The church leaders see 1 out of 10 attenders sometime during the year for more than one session of counseling (couples count as two).

5 _____ The church leaders see 1 out of 15 attenders or less sometime during the year for more than one session of counseling (couples count as two).

Restoration Process

1 _____ The church has never practiced a restoration process with people who fall into sin.

2 _____ The only restoration processes the church has had has been done by the pastor.

3 _____ The restoration process in the church is led by the pastor and the leaders only.

4 _____ The pastor has trained a lay team to lead in the restoration process.

5 _____   The majority of the restoration processes are initiated by lay people in the church, either through the shepherds or through the leaders of small groups.

Leader

1 _____   System is either led by the pastor, his wife or is not assigned.

2 _____   System is led by an untrained volunteer.

3 _____   System is led by a trained leader over volunteers.

4 _____   System is led by a dedicated leader who is overseeing a team of leaders.

5 _____   System is led by a dedicated leader who is overseeing a team and also mentoring his or her replacement.

Bonus Points

+1 _____   The church engages in a yearly special time/retreat of spiritual renewal through spiritual practices apart from preaching.

+1 _____   The church has a grace model of transformational training process.

+3 _____   The church has a clear grace model of transformational training process through which over 50% of the attenders have gone.

Total _____ divided by 5 = _____

Vision System Evaluation

Healthy Outcome: We are united and moving forward towards accomplishing a common godly purpose.

Written Vision

1 _____ The church has no clarifying vision statement that defines the reason God has us in this community.

2 _____ A survey of the congregation indicates that less than 10% can recite the vision statement.

3 _____ A survey of the congregation indicates at least 25% know the vision of the church.

4 _____ A survey of the congregation indicates more than 50% know the vision of the church.

5 _____ A survey of the congregation indicates more than 75% know the vision of the church.

Written Strategy

1 _____ The church has no written strategy for implementing our vision.

2 _____ The church has a written strategy for implementing this vision, but less than 25% of our ministries are aligned with our vision.

3 _____ The church has a written strategy for implementing this vision, but less than 50% of our ministries are aligned with our vision.

4 _____ The church has a written strategy for implementing this vision and 50-75% of our ministries align with our vision.

5 _____ The church has a written strategy for implementing this vision and more than 75% of our ministries align with our vision.

Ministry Evaluation

1 _____ The church does not practice a yearly ministry evaluation process to make sure that our ministries are aligned with the vision.

3 _____ The church practices a ministry evaluation process every other year to make sure that our ministries are aligned with the vision.

5 _____ The church practices a yearly ministry evaluation process to make sure

that our ministries are aligned with the vision.

Evaluation Markers

1 _____ The church has no way to evaluate our ministries against strategy.

2 _____ The church is hitting less than 25% of our evaluation markers.

3 _____ The church is hitting at least 25-50% of our yearly evaluation markers.

4 _____ The church is hitting at least 50-75% of our yearly evaluation markers.

5 _____ The church is hitting at least 75-90% of our yearly evaluation markers.

Celebration

1 _____ The church does not have any focused celebration over achieving our vision strategy.

2 _____ The church has at least one planned celebration time a year over achieving our vision strategy.

3 _____ The church has three to five celebration times a year over achieving some aspect of our vision strategy.

4 _____ The church has a monthly celebration over achieving some aspect of our vision strategy.

5 _____ The church has a weekly celebration over achieving some aspect of our vision strategy.

Growth

1 _____ The church experienced less than 5% growth in each of the last three years.

2 _____ The church experienced 5% growth for one year out of the last three years.

3 _____ The church experienced 5% growth for each of the last three years.

4 _____ The church experienced 10% growth for one year out of the last three years.

5 _____ The church has experienced 10%+ growth for each of the last three years.

Total _____ **divided by 6 =** _____

Evangelizing System Evaluation

Healthy Outcome: Disciples are regularly witnessing to others, resulting in consistent conversion growth in the church.

Training Participation

1 _____   Except for a few individuals, no one has been trained in evangelism nor is a training class offered.

2 _____   A training class in evangelism is offered at least once a year, with 10% of the congregation having been through the training.

3 _____   25% of the congregation has been through the church's training process on evangelism.

4 _____   50% of the congregation has been through the church's training process on evangelism.

5 _____   More than 75% of the congregation has been through the church's training process on evangelism.

Conversion Growth

1 _____   Aside from baptizing children of members, yearly conversion growth is less than 1 person baptized per 50 members per year.

2 _____   Yearly conversion growth is 1 person baptized per 50 members.

3 _____   Yearly conversion growth is 1 person baptized per 30 members.

4 _____   Yearly conversion growth is 1 person baptized per 20 members.

5 _____   Yearly conversion growth is more than 1 person baptized per 10 members.

Retention (those who do not move from the community)

1 _____   The church has retained less than 25% of new believers over the last five years.

2 _____   The church has retained between 25-49% of new believers over the last five years.

3 _____   The church has retained between 50-74% of new believers over the last five years.

4 _____   The church has retained between 75-98% of new believers over the last five years.

5 _____   The church has retained more than 90% of new believers over the last five years.

Discipleship

1 _____   The church has no process for moving new believers from baptism to discipleship.

2 _____   Up to 25% of the new believers have entered our discipleship process.

3 _____   Up to 50% of the new believers have entered our discipleship process.

4 _____   Up to 75% of the new believers have entered our discipleship process.

5 _____   Up to 90% or more of the new believers have entered our discipleship process.

Leader

1 _____   System is either led by the pastor, his wife or is not assigned.

2 _____   System is led by an untrained volunteer.

3 _____   System is led by a trained leader over volunteers.

4 _____   System is led by a dedicated leader who is overseeing a team of leaders.

5 _____   System is led by a dedicated leader who is overseeing a team and also mentoring his or her replacement.

Total _____ divided by 5 = _____

Discipling System Evaluation

Healthy Outcome: Disciples are pursuing God, conforming to the likeness of Jesus and growing into co-workers in the Kingdom.

Process

1 _____   The church has no defined process of discipling new believers.

2 _____   The church has a 3-6 month discipling process developed for new believers.

3 _____   The church has a 9-15 month discipling process developed for new believers.

4 _____   The church has an 18-24 month discipling process developed for new believers.

5 _____   The church has implemented a discipling process for teens and children.

Content

1 _____   There are no designated courses that new disciples are expected to take.

2 _____   Disciples are offered Christian life courses and Bible classes.

3 _____   Disciples are expected to take entry level biblical and theological knowledge courses.

4 _____   Disciples are expected to take entry level spiritual transformation foundations training as well as the biblical and theological knowledge courses.

5 _____   Entry level and advanced spiritual transformation and biblical knowledge/world view training is offered.

New Believer Participation

1 _____   Over the last five years, less than 25% of new believers received some kind of discipling.

2 _____   Over the last five years, 25-49% of new believers have entered into this process.

3 _____   Over the last five years, 50-74% of new believers have entered into this process.

4 ____   Over the last five years, 75-89% of new believers have entered into this process.

5 ____   Over the last five years, more than 90% of new believers have entered into this process.

Mature Believer Participation

1 ____   The pastor and his wife engage in discipling new believers.

2 ____   The pastor and a few leaders of the church disciple new believers.

3 ____   10% of the members are trained and are engaged in discipling new believers.

4 ____   30% of the members are trained and are engaged in discipling new believers.

5 ____   50% of the members are trained and are engaged in discipling new believers.

Leader

1 ____   System is either led by the pastor, his wife or is not assigned.

2 ____   System is led by an untrained volunteer.

3 ____   System is led by a trained leader over volunteers.

4 ____   System is led by a dedicated leader who is overseeing a team of leaders.

5 ____   System is led by a dedicated leader who is overseeing a team and also mentoring his or her replacement.

Total _____ divided by 5 = _____

Leadership Training System Evaluation

Healthy Outcome: Future leaders are continually being identified and prepared to lead.

Process

1 _____ The church has no defined leadership training process.

2 _____ The church has classes in leadership training.

3 _____ The church has a mentoring process or a monthly gathering for leaders as well as leadership training classes.

4 _____ The church has a monthly gathering of leaders and a mentoring process as well as leadership training classes.

5 _____ In addition to a monthly gathering, mentoring and basic leadership classes, the church offers advanced classes in leadership.

Where Leaders Come From

1 _____ 90% of our new leaders come from members who transferred into the church from another church.

2 _____ 20% of our new leaders are people who came to faith through this church.

3 _____ 30% of our new leaders are people who came to faith through this church.

4 _____ 40% of our new leaders are people who came to faith through this church.

5 _____ 50% of our new leaders are people who came to faith through this church.

Total New Leaders Per Year

1 _____ The church rarely develops and deploys new leaders.

2 _____ The church develops less than 1% of attenders as new leaders every year,

3 _____ The church develops up to 3% of attenders as new leaders every year,

4 _____ The church develops up to 7% of attenders as new leaders every year, which has allowed us to expand our Growth Systems (Small Groups, Ministries, Missions) into new areas.

5 _____   The church develops 10% of attenders as new leaders every year, which allows us to send out leaders to help start a new congregation.

Age of New Leaders

1 _____   More than 60% of new leaders are older than 45.

2 _____   More than 50% of new leaders are older than 45.

3 _____   60% of new leaders are under 45 years old.

4 _____   40% of new leaders are under 35 years old.

5 _____   40% of new leaders are under 25 years old, 10% being in their teens.

Leader

1 _____   System is either led by the pastor, his wife or is not assigned.

2 _____   System is led by an untrained volunteer.

3 _____   System is led by a trained leader over volunteers.

4 _____   System is led by a dedicated leader who is overseeing a team of leaders.

5 _____   System is led by a dedicated leader who is overseeing a team and also mentoring his or her replacement.

Total _____ divided by 5 = _____

Final Evaluation

Write the total from the five sections below. Compare your church's totals to the corresponding health category. If you find that only one or two are in the unhealthy or surviving category, rebuilding these systems will be your focus going forward. If there are 3 or more, especially if all five fall into these categories, your church needs serious help.

	Totals	Unhealthy	Surviving	Stable	Significant
Spiritual Life	_____	2.1 or less	2.2 – 3.0	3.1 – 4.0	4.1+
Vision	_____	2.1 or less	2.2 – 3.0	3.1 – 4.0	4.1+
Evangelizing	_____	2.1 or less	2.2 – 3.0	3.1 – 4.0	4.1+
Discipling	_____	2.1 or less	2.2 – 3.0	3.1 – 4.0	4.1+
Leadership Training	_____	2.1 or less	2.2 – 3.0	3.1 – 4.0	4.1+

Unhealthy indicates that this system is in a bad state, causing the church to fail to make and retain more disciples.

Surviving means that the system is passable, but that it is probably undermining other systems that are dependent on it.

Stable signifies this system is an asset to your church's health. The more systems in the stable range, the more likely the church is growing.

Significant is when your church is doing this system so well that you may now be influencing other congregations who have come to learn from you.

Where Do You Go from Here?

If you are facing the challenge of rebuilding some or all of these Five Critical Systems, understand that they must be addressed in the order they appear. These five follow a sequence, with the first system providing the foundation for the next and so on. Healthy spiritual life leads to being ready to hear a vision from God. A healthy vision from God gives the congregation a passion to evangelize the lost around them. An influx of newly minted believers gives you people to disciple. Discipled believers supply potential new leaders to train. Your church is then ready to grow.

You cannot jump into the middle of the sequence and expect to produce a healthy system. While you can prepare a system for healthy evangelizing or discipling, how effective will these systems be if your congregation does not even see the lost who need the gospel? Or what value is pursuing a vision from God when your congregation's heart is not turned toward God? Following the sequence will get you to your goal of a healthy congregation, even of it takes longer than you think it should.

You will need a coach to help you. Since there are a lot of things you never learned in seminary, you will need help grasping how and why new ideas will or will not work for your congregation.

You will also need information. Your next step could be reading *Increasing Church Capacity Primer: Learn to Think in Systems* by Dr. Steve Smith, which will introduce you to systemic thinking and give you an overview of each ministry system your church needs. It includes a complete evaluation for each of the 18 church ministry systems. Another book which goes deeper into the Five Critical Systems is *Church GameChanger: Five Essentials for Revitalization* by Dr. Steve Smith.

If you choose to pursue a coach, you will need *The Increasing Church Capacity Guidebook: Developing and Linking the 18 Systems* which is included as part of complete video Systems Training Package by Dr. Steve Smith. This guidebook is unlike other resources which are heavy on reading. It is a practical step-by-step workbook for building each of the ministry systems you need, asking you to define your theology and answer pertinent questions so you can design each system to fit your congregation.

The videos give detailed instruction for each module of the Guidebook. You can find it at www.churchequippers.com/store

Bonus Chapter: Why Healthy Churches Led by Healthy Pastors Stay Under 100 People

Not every smaller church is in desperate straits. Many are quite healthy and loving toward God and the people who need Him. You may be leading one of these churches. And you still wonder why it is that the church is not growing. You just tested your critical systems and did not see indications that any were a serious problem. Your congregation's spiritual life is healthy, the vision is clear, the church sows the gospel to the community readily, you have a good discipleship process in place and you are seeing new leaders emerging. But you still cannot crack the 200 level in attendance.

What I know from observing pastors and reading about church leadership over the last 30 plus years is that this is a common problem. Research tells us that attendance in 60% of all American churches is 100 people or less, and 85% of all churches are attended by fewer than 200. Plenty of pastors are concerned enough to attend a seminar or seek training or read a book on how to break the 200 barrier.

But let me suggest that lack of knowledge is not the issue. The real issue most of the time is the Connection System. By that I mean you, the pastor, are the problematic Connection System. And it is questionable whether this will change unless you face it. Even then it may not change.

Here is what I see all the time. In many congregations everyone is connected to the pastor. He has a high touch shepherd style. He is the person they call when they are in need, go to when they want counsel, ask to visit and spend time with them when they are free. He checks on them when they are missing in action at church. He visits them when they are in the hospital. He works at knowing their concerns and being involved with their children and teens. He does all the preaching, marrying and burying. This is not seen as a problem because he loves ministering to the needs of his congregation. He wants them to feel he is available 24/7.

Let's look at the following scenario. A new family comes to visit the church. The high touch shepherd has two options available to him at that point. The first is that he can take time away from someone who is already connected with the congregation and give it to the new family so they will stay. But this comes with a cost.

Studies show that people have only so many personal relationships they can maintain in their lives. This is also true for pastors. The pastor may have anywhere from 40 to 60 relationship slots. When they are full, he is at capacity. This means that when the church reaches 50-100 people (total number of his personal relationships plus their family members), he is operating at his maximum relationship range. There are certain pastors that can stretch the upper range to 80 or more relationships, but often those relationships are not as deep or the pastor is robbing family time to supply the extra relationship hours required.

Now back to the scenario. The pastor takes time away from an already connected person to try to draw in the new family. The new family responds well. They love the way the pastor is investing in them. But the attender that just lost his or her allotted time with the pastor will begin to unconsciously feel deserted and alienation will set in. Before long, that person will leave the congregation and the newbie will become the regular attender. The size of the congregation gains and loses ground consistently by this approach.

Or the pastor will choose the second option. He has no more relationship slots open, so therefore has no time to invest to draw in the new family. He will hope that others in the congregation offer the needed connection for this new family to stay. But the culture of the congregation is fixed. The pastor is the connection system. The statistics point to the probability that visitors also come from that kind of church background. Not getting the expected shepherding attention from the pastor means they will not stay. The church experiences a short bump in its average attendance, but does not grow.

Not everyone says this out loud, but you may have heard those departing your congregation share the expression, "I am not getting my needs met." You might think they are speaking about spiritual needs, but they are really speaking about not getting their basic relationship needs filled by you, the pastor. Many people confuse the two needs because they do not understand the difference. So, they believe it when they say that you or the church are unspiritual even though spirituality has nothing to do with it.

Here is what you have to face. You may be unwilling to change your style of pastoring to grow the church larger. I know numerous pastors who are convinced that being a high touch shepherd is their calling from God. They still wish the church would grow larger, but they cannot stop being what they are, nor deep down do they desire to change. They will continue to pastor churches in the 50-100 range for all of their ministry years. If this is you, be assured that there is nothing wrong with you. This is how you are wired by God. Take joy in your calling.

But what if you are a high touch shepherd and do want to change? What can you do? Your ministry model has been to make sure people's needs are met, that each has someone to personally invest in their lives, and that person is *you*. Can you change your ways?

There is only one way to address this. You can only change your ways by changing your mind about what you are called to do as a pastor. And this will not be easy. You must adopt the role as the *trainer of lay shepherds* rather than the personal shepherd of each attender. It will be the lay shepherds who will give attention to the shepherding needs of most of the attenders, while you invest in the lives of your leaders. In doing this you will increase the number of connection points for your church.

But be aware that when you start this process, it may, and probably will, cause some close personal friends to leave your congregation. They want to be connected to the pastor and nothing else will do for them. They learned this from their church culture, which you have reinforced by your ministry style.

Also know that this change will be hard on you emotionally in the beginning. You will feel this most when others you train are rewarded with the trust from those they have begun to shepherd that you alone used to have. Your emotions will want to pull you back into the role to which you are most accustomed. But recognize that this change is not about neglecting those you pastor. It is about freeing yourself to be a different kind of pastor, one who can lead this congregation toward a larger impact on your community.

Change is hard. But it is possible. If you are willing to change and want to learn how to lead this way, you will need a coach to help you. Coaching may be available through your regional church overseer. Coach training is available through Church Equippers at ChurchEquippers.com. Encourage your regional leader to contact Church Equippers. If coaching is not available to you, you may request coaching through Church Equippers at our website, or just feel free to give us a call to chat about your situation without any obligation at (863)-698-0428.

About the Author

Dr. Steve Smith has a passion for God and for the gospel of Jesus Christ that transforms lives. He has served as pastor, church planter, regional church overseer, trainer, coach, and mentor to pastors during his career which began in 1982. He has developed unique tools and a new model to help pastors and churches become healthy in order to make and retain more disciples.

Steve is a biblical "nuts and bolts" kind of guy. His conversational, down-to-earth style of speaking and writing makes his concepts accessible to anyone no matter their level of education or experience.

He is currently coaching pastors and their implementers across multiple church denominations toward revitalization. He is also training teams of coaches within church networks to help other pastors to revitalize their own churches. Video training is also available through ChurchEquippers.com.

Born in Virginia, Steve is an extensive reader and has wide interests, including history, travel, trivia, the Shenandoah Valley of Virginia and Sudoku. Married for over 40 years to his wife, Shirley, they have 4 children and 5 grandchildren. Their home base is in central Florida.

OTHER PUBLICATIONS

- *Church GameChanger: Five Essentials for Revitalization*
- *The Increasing Church Capacity Guidebook: Designing and Linking the 18 Systems*
- *Increasing Church Capacity Primer: Learn to Think in Systems*
- *The Key to Deep Change: Experiencing Spiritual Transformation by Facing Unfinished Business* (also available in Spanish)
- *Key to Deep Change Study: Small Group Experience Small Group Guide/Leader's Guide* (also available in Spanish)
- *Restart: Escaping Anxiety and Fear* for young adults and teens
- *Build Deep: Developing a Transformational Culture in Your Church*

CE

Church Equippers